AN OCTOPUS

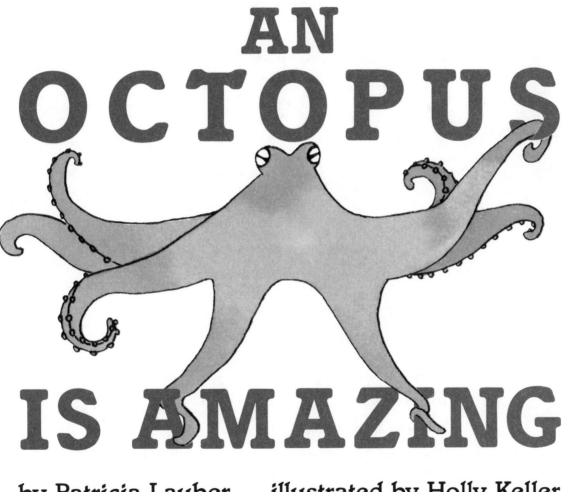

IS AMAZING

by Patricia Lauber   illustrated by Holly Keller

Thomas Y. Crowell   New York

LET'S READ-AND-FIND-OUT BOOK CLUB EDITION

The *Let's-Read-and-Find-Out Science Book* series was originated by Dr. Franklyn M. Branley, Astronomer Emeritus and former Chairman of the American Museum–Hayden Planetarium, and was formerly co-edited by him and Dr. Roma Gans, Professor Emeritus of Childhood Education, Teachers College, Columbia University.

Let's-Read-and-Find-Out Science Book is a registered
trademark of Harper & Row, Publishers, Inc.

AN OCTOPUS IS AMAZING
Text copyright © 1990 by Patricia G. Lauber
Illustrations copyright © 1990 by Holly Keller
Printed in the U.S.A. All rights reserved.
Typography by Elynn Cohen
1   2   3   4   5   6   7   8   9   10
First Edition

Library of Congress Cataloging-in-Publication Data
Lauber, Patricia.
   An Octopus is amazing / by Patricia Lauber ; illustrated by Holly
Keller.
     p.   cm. — (A Let's-read-and-find-out science book)
   Summary: An introduction to one of the curiosities of the sea—the
multi-tentacled, highly intelligent octopus.
   ISBN 0-690-04801-7 : $. — ISBN 0-690-04803-3 (lib. bdg.) :
$
   1. Octopus—Juvenile literature. [1. Octopus.] I. Keller,
Holly, ill. II. Title. III. Series.
QL430.3.02L38 1990   89-29300
594'.56—dc20   CIP
                                          AC

AN OCTOPUS IS AMAZING

THERE ARE MORE THAN 150 KNOWN KINDS OF OCTOPUS

GIANT OCTOPUS
Length: up to 17 feet
Weight: up to 110 pounds
Found in temperate waters of the northern
Pacific, from California to Japan.

COMMON OCTOPUS
Length: up to 30 inches
Weight: from 2 to 4 pounds
Found all over the world in tropical
to temperate waters.

BLUE-RINGED OCTOPUS
Length: from 1½ to 3 inches
Weight: from 2 to 3 ounces
Found in tropical waters near Australia and
Indonesia. It is the only octopus whose bite
is poisonous to humans.

DWARF OCTOPUS
Length: 4 inches
Weight: ½ ounce
Found in Caribbean waters, this tiny
octopus is a popular choice for home
aquariums.

How to Measure an Octopus

Measure length from tip of bag
to tip of arm

An octopus is an animal that lives in the sea. It has a soft, bag-shaped body and eight rubbery arms.

The common octopus lives in a den near shore. It may make its den in a cave or a wrecked ship, in a shell or a tin can, under a rock or in a crack in a rock.

Every octopus lives alone. Its den is small, just big enough to hold the octopus. An octopus can squeeze into a small space because it has no backbone. In fact, it has no bones at all.

An octopus can change color in a flash.

Usually the octopus matches its surroundings and is hard to see. If it climbs into an empty shell, it turns pink and gray. If it crawls among rocks and seaweeds, it may turn brown and gray and green.

An octopus can have colored spots or stripes. It can be half one color and half another.

Color changes help an octopus to hide or to escape from enemies. They may also show how an octopus is feeling. Scientists say an angry octopus turns dark red. A frightened one turns pale. An octopus that is enjoying a meal shows pleasure by changing color.

An octopus has a big appetite. Crabs are its favorite food, but it also likes lobsters, clams, and other shellfish. Sometimes an octopus waits in its den until a meal passes by. Then it reaches out an arm and grabs.

Each arm is lined with suckers. They work like little rubber suction cups. The common octopus has 240 suckers on each arm.

The octopus holds its food with its suckers and examines it.

The octopus carries its catch toward its mouth. The mouth is on the underside of the body, and inside it is a hard, curved beak. The octopus uses its beak to crack the shell of its prey. It squirts the prey with poison from a gland in its mouth. When the prey is paralyzed or dead, the octopus feeds.

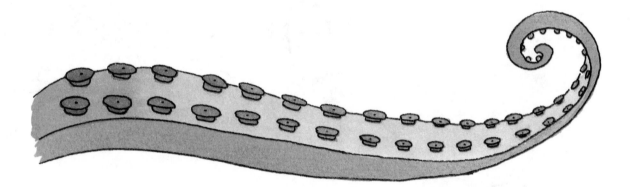

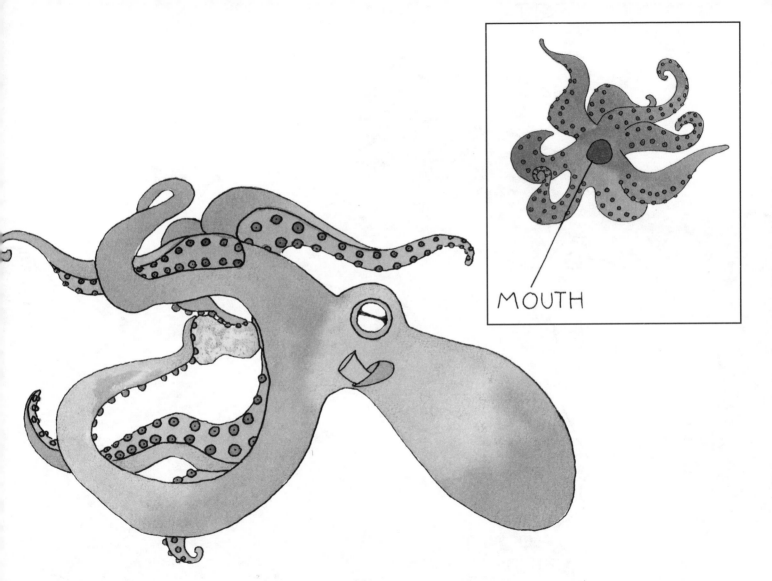

MOUTH

Sometimes an octopus leaves its den and hunts for food. It hunts by sight, using its sharp eyes.

The octopus may crawl along, using its suckers to hold on to rocks and pulling itself forward.

Or it may jet, by drawing in water and shooting it out through a tube, which is called the siphon. With each spurt, the octopus jets through the sea.

Once the octopus spies something to eat, it spreads its webbed arms. It floats down and wraps itself around its prey. It may store crabs or clams in its suckers and take them home to eat.

When an octopus has eaten, it tidies up its den. It
clears out the shells, using its siphon to blow them away.

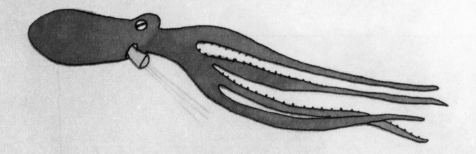

Sometimes other animals try to eat an octopus. The octopus does not fight. Instead, it tries to hide or escape.

If a big fish attacks, the octopus changes colors and jets off. The octopus no longer looks like the animal the fish was going to attack. And so the fish is fooled.

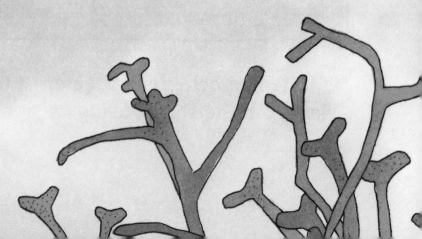

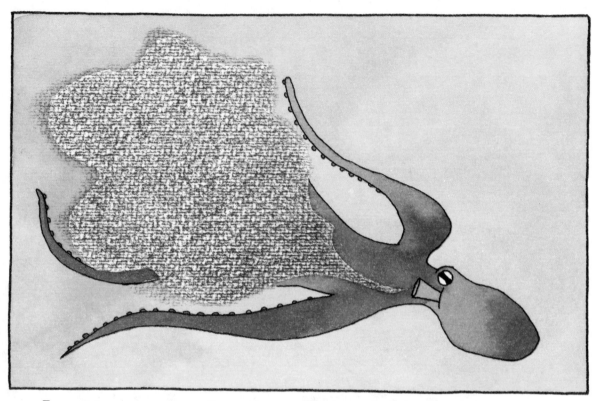

An octopus can also give off an ink-black liquid through its siphon. The ink forms a blob that has the shape and smell of an octopus. The enemy attacks the blob. The octopus, which has turned black, escapes.

That is how an octopus defends itself against the moray eel, one of its most dangerous enemies. A moray eel is big enough to swallow an octopus whole. It has sharp teeth and a keen sense of smell, which it uses in hunting.

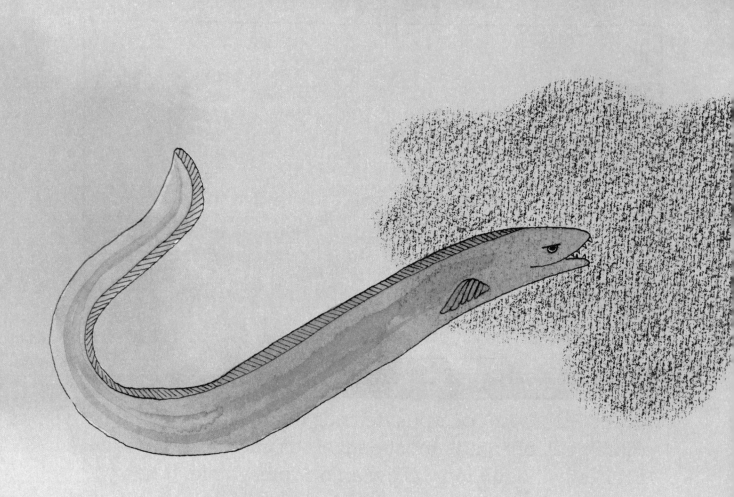

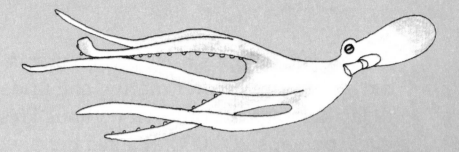

When an octopus sees a moray, it turns black and gives off a blob of ink.

The moray picks up the scent of the black blob and attacks it. The octopus turns white and jets away.

Sometimes a moray eel is able to tear off one of the octopus' arms before the octopus escapes. If this happens, the octopus can hunt and travel with seven arms. And in time, it grows a new arm.

A female octopus mates when she is one to two years old. A few weeks after mating she finds a den and starts to lay her eggs. A common octopus lays thousands of eggs, perhaps 200,000. It takes her a week or more to lay them.

Each egg is the size of half a grain of rice and has a stem. The female weaves and glues the stems together, making strings about four inches long. She hangs the strings in her den.

From then on, the female spends all her time taking care of her eggs. She does not hunt or eat.

The eggs take four to six weeks or more to hatch. The female guards them from hungry fishes. She keeps the water around the eggs fresh and clean by blowing on the strings and running her arms through them. When the eggs hatch, the female's job is done and she dies.

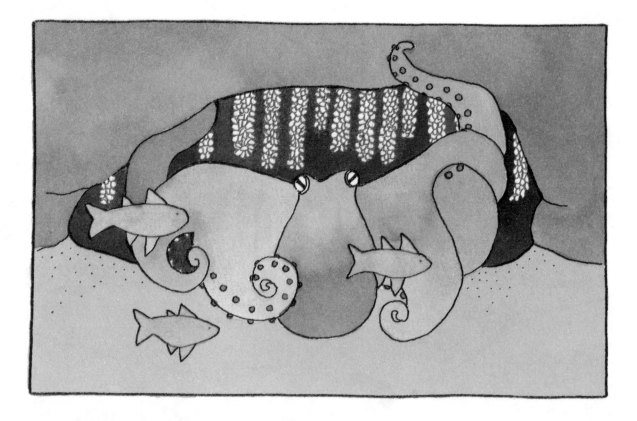

The newly hatched young are tiny, no bigger than fleas. They can change color and give off ink, but they cannot jet or crawl or hide in dens. For a month or more they drift in the sea. Most become food for fishes and other animals. Only a few live to grow up. As they do, they become surprisingly clever animals.

Long ago, people learned that an octopus is good at solving problems. If an octopus cannot open a clam, it waits for the clam to open itself. Then it places a pebble between the two shells. The clam can no longer close up tight, and the octopus eats it.

If an octopus is given a glass jar with a crab inside, it tries to get at the crab. After a few tries, it solves the problem. It takes the top off the jar.

Being able to solve problems is a sign of intelligence.

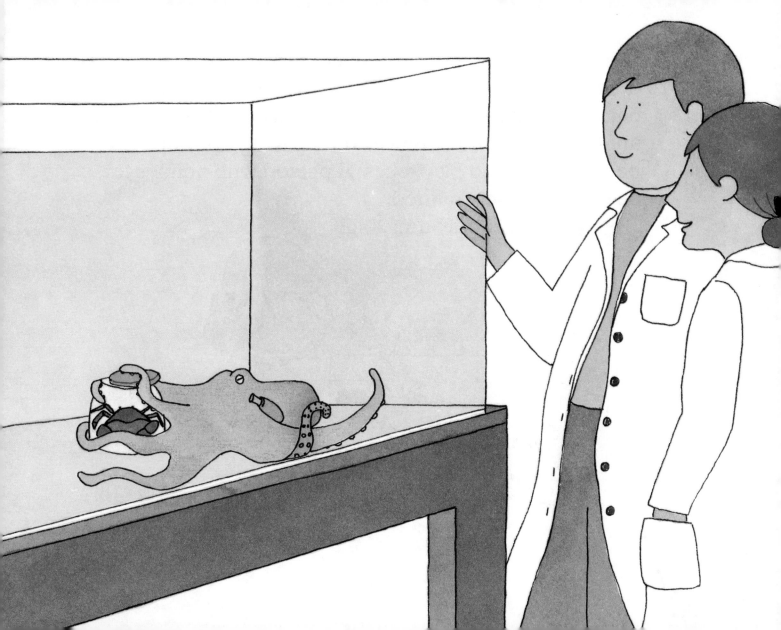

In the wild, octopuses are shy. In aquariums and labs they seem to like the people they get to know. They enjoy being stroked. And they are playful. Playfulness is another sign of intelligence. They play tug-of-war with people. They also play jokes. A person who annoys an octopus may get squirted.

An octopus is truly amazing.